11

P9-DCR-647

Drama Games

FOR

Children

Fun and Learning
with Acting and Make-Believe

Paul Rooyackers

Illustrated by Cecilia Bowman

a Hunter House SmartFun book

Hunter House Inc., Publishers
P O Box 2914
Alameda CA 94501-0914

Library of Congress Cataloging-in-Publication Data

Rooyackers, Paul.
[Honderd dramaspelen. English]
101 drama games for children : fun and learning with acting and make-believe / by Paul Rooyackers. — 1st ed.
p. cm.
"First published in The Netherlands in 1993 by Panta Rhei as Honderd dramaspelen" —T.p. verso.
"A Hunter House smartfun book."
Includes bibliographical references (p.).
ISBN 0-89793-211-0 (pbk.) — ISBN 0-89793-212-9 (spiral)
1. Games. 2. Drama. I. Title.
GV1203.R58813   1997
790.1'922—dc21   97-20957
                                  CIP

Ordering

Hunter House books are available at bulk discounts for textbook course adoptions; to qualifying community, healthcare, and government organizations; and for special promotions and fundraising. For details please contact:

Special Sales Department
Hunter House Inc., PO Box 2914, Alameda CA 94501-0914
Tel. (510) 865-5282 Fax (510) 865-4295
e-mail: marketing@hunterhouse.com
Individuals can order our books from most bookstores or by calling toll-free:
1-800-266-5592
....

Project Coordinator: Wendy Low   Production: Paul Frindt
Cover Design: Jil Weil Graphic Design   Book Design: Dian-Aziza Ooka
Illustrations: Cecilia Bowman   Translated by: Panta Rhei Katwijk
Copy Editors: Rosemary Wallner, Dana Weissman   Proofreader: Lee Rappold
Editorial Coordinators: Dana Weissman, Belinda Breyer
Marketing Director: Corrine M. Sahli   Marketing Associate: Susan Markey
Customer Support: Christina Arciniega, Edgar M. Estavilla, Jr.
Order fulfillment: A & A Quality Shipping Services
Publisher: Kiran S. Rana
....

Printed and Bound by Data Reproductions, Auburn Hills, MI
Manufactured in the United States of America

9 8 7 6 5 4 3 2   First Edition

101 Drama Games
for Children

Other SmartFun Books:

101 Music Games by Jerry Storms

101 Dance Games by Paul Rooyackers

Contents

*A detailed list of games with appropriate age levels
starts on the next page.*

List of Games

List of Games, continued

List of Games, continued

List of Games, continued

List of Games, continued

101 Drama Games
for Children

Preface

The concept of drama *games* is a new one. The terms *drama* and *play* are closely related. In this book, drama and play complement each other and merge into a new activity: the drama game.

The drama games in this book are for teachers and group leaders who work with children both within and outside mainstream education. Feel free to adapt any of these games to regular school activities; as independent projects, they can easily be developed into dramatic performances.

The book consists of two parts. The first part, "Drama and Play," explains what is meant here by the words *drama, play* and *game*. You'll also find explanations of a drama game's elements and how a game develops into a performance. You'll read about your role as leader and about how drama games can play a part in the social development of group members. Also covered are ways to select games, to systematically prepare for them, to organize a group, and to build the activity to a satisfying conclusion.

The second part, "Let's Act," contains the drama games divided into ten sections, each based on a certain theme or use of materials. An introduction before each division provides explanations and helpful hints. The games in each section gradually increase in difficulty. You can combine games from different sections for workshops or other extended activities.

All of these drama games have been developed in actual groups and classes, and have proven their value. Players with little dramatic experience can enjoy all the games; however, you as the teacher or group leader should try out a game before using it with a group.

Over the years I have invented and adapted an array of drama games with the cooperation of many participants with whom I have worked in schools and on projects. This book is dedicated to them and to all the enthusiasts, young and old, from whom I have benefited.

Best of luck!

Paul Rooyackers
The Netherlands, 1997

Drama and Play

Linking Drama with Play

Play is an important activity. Everyone's youth begins with and is enriched by it. During play you escape from reality and behave as if everything is different. For a moment you become someone else and experience how that feels. During play you can make mistakes and try things that you wouldn't dare do in every day life. The use of fantasy in play is not just for small children. Adults also enjoy the chance to escape from reality from time to time—to relax and climb inside the skin of another character. Yet playing is often also reflective of your experience, of your life.

In a drama game, you inhabit a world different from the one in which you live. You use your imagination to portray or dramatize something. By your actions, you show others what you want to portray. Acting out what you have prepared is a very important part of drama games.

You can build games using dance, drama, art, music, sports, or other types of activity. The word *act* comes from the Latin word meaning "to do." Players perform acts on stage. These actions portray planned—and improvised—situations. Actors express themselves through their bodies and through language. For example, an actor may move like a ghost, making all kinds of strange sounds. Or he may be a farmer on a tractor, bumping back and forth across a field. Or he may act out a pleasant or scary situation he's heard about or experienced.

Two means of expression are linked together in this book: drama and play. Combining these two activities produces a *drama game* in which the group experiences the prepared game through demonstrating it to one another.

These games should not be confused with formal performances on a raised stage in front of an audience. You and your group can play these drama games in any kind of space and at any level of proficiency. It is *play*, not theater. The difference between these games and regular play is that here you try to give the games *form*. Players practice not only how to play with others but also how to give their actions a dramatic form. Players tell and act out stories and experiences, what they find important about a situation, how they think and feel about it, and how they want to translate it into a drama game. They make agreements with each other: Everyone knows that the others have prepared something and that they are going to act out something that they have imagined.

Why Use Drama Games?

Drama games are relaxing. Relaxation is an extremely important aspect of play, and enjoying a game is of prime importance—but that doesn't mean you always have to laugh to enjoy another's performance. A serious subject can give just as much pleasure as a humorous one. If you don't feel comfortable and at ease with the others in the group and if you can't freely express you opinions, a drama game is not possible. You won't want to take part if you feel restrained by another person or the situation.

Drama games develop your creativity. In a drama game, you explore the world around you. You act and tell stories with others, and this is informative. You learn to get along with others and to develop ideas both with others and by yourself. Through play you learn to see self-expression, subjects, themes, and the other players in a new way. These experiences expand your ability to play, and help you in daily life to manage thoughts and problems more creatively.

Drama games develop your personality. You learn to work with your imagination and process your experiences consciously in your way of relating to others. You gain more control over what you say and do and how you move. Your self-esteem grows through playing.

Drama games contribute to social and emotional development. You can learn how to handle situations by acting them out, by exploring how you would react to and behave in such situations. Playing expands your knowledge of yourself: you can dare to say more about things, partly through language but also through physical expression. You can help another person in the game. Not everyone is able to discover the truth of every situation by themselves or change their point of view on particular points. Play works like a mirror; you discover what you are able to do. Play also teaches you to concentrate better on a particular situation or assignment. Players experience each other differently in play than in every day life. They learn to trust and evaluate themselves and others better.

Drama games improve your composition skills. If you show a dramatization to other people, it is important that they understand the story. It is important to understand how the play will come across visually: has the game been well thought out with regard to form and content? You must put sufficient effort into a game to make it enjoyable to watch, so that others will enjoy your way of playing, telling a story, moving, and imagining. Certain props can be included in the presentation.

Drama games develop oral and physical expression. You learn to express yourself better through playing, because you learn new words and different ways of speaking and communicating.

The same applies to your use of your body during and after the game. In a drama game players tend to stand closer to other people than they would in daily life. They interact with others more directly, have more physical contact with each other, and so learn how to deal with these unfamiliar situations.

What Can I Do to Link Drama and Play?

The Role of the Leader

Prepare the sessions. As the leader, you prepare each session in advance. This includes deciding how you will present the games; where the class will be held; in what kind of space; at what time of day. How large is the group and is it already experienced with this type of game? Is the size of the work space suitable for the size of the group? You must create a suitable space and gather props. More importantly, you stimulate the players, guide the assignments, and keep an eye on the whole process. And finally, you must have an idea of how the game should be completed and, as far as is appropriate, steer it in that direction.

Speak loudly and clearly. Introducing a game to the players is an important part of the process. If the players can't hear or understand the instructions completely, the game will not work well. The warmth and inspiration in your voice can contribute to a better development of the game. The volume of your voice, its power, its intonation, and correctly chosen words all help to stimulate the group to practice and perform the game. You talk the players into the process.

Keep the game on track. Watch and listen to group members and anticipate what could happen. It is important to recognize when a game is going in a direction other than the one you planned. Step in and make suggestions so that the game does not suddenly go flat. The players also may have ideas that they would like to express; the greater their experience the more ideas they will have. Take their opinions into account when giving your suggestions. A good leader knows the level that the players have reached and adjusts the game accordingly. Use a positive approach toward group members; this will have a positive effect on the game itself.

Adjust the game to suit your group of players. As the leader you will be able to see whether an adjustment can be accomplished immediately or whether you need to make a shift during the course of the game. Observe the players and decide what adaptations are needed: should you change the group's size or makeup? Have you correctly estimated the ability of the players? Can the group relate to the theme sufficiently?

Observe the players. As you watch the players, consider whether this is an activity that they will want to do again.

During the game, stimulate the players in such a way that they will look forward to the next session. The stimulation you give can enhance their concentration, their spontaneity, their joy in playing, and their involvement in the content of the assignments. Notice the ways players work with each other, observe the ways they make contributions, and, whether they seem able to make use of their experience during and after the class.

Know the players and their abilities. Try to become familiar with the group ahead of time. Know their ages and their strengths—there is a huge difference between a group made up only of boys or only girls and a mixed group. With a new group, get a sense of their abilities and adapt quickly. A drama game can be an intense experience. Keep this in mind when working with a new group, and be sensitive to players' different life experiences.

Choosing a Drama Game

When you have sufficient information about the players and the situation in which you will be working, you can give more thought to the content of the program. Look through the games in the second section, "Let's Act," and choose a game (or games) that seems suitable. Ask yourself why you want to use a particular game. What is it that you want to teach or tell the players? What do you want them to experience?

When putting a program together, keep the following points in mind:

- Try out any drama game before presenting it to a group.

- Take time to prepare the game; you must be able to visualize the way the game will develop and see where problems could arise.

- Present the game briefly and clearly, and demonstrate as you describe the assignment.

- Based on your experience with the group, develop a

plan to begin the series of drama games and get the group going.

- Plan the order of the games so that they follow each other logically.

- Have a good overview of the game and be able to guide it from various positions in the room.

- Agree with the group about how you will intervene if you see that the game is going off on a tangent.

- Distribute the roles evenly and watch how the players work together as a group and in subgroups.

- Be aware in advance of the emotions the drama game may bring out in the players.

- Be aware of how you bring the game to a conclusion. Try to estimate the extent to which everyone can benefit from the drama game emotionally and technically.

How to Use This Book

Part Two, "Let's Act," contains ten different types of games to try with your group. Use combinations of games and adapt each to fit your group's theme or subject. To help you find games suitable for a particular group and time period, all the games are coded with symbols or icons. These icons tell you at a glance some things about the game:

the appropriate age group

the amount of time needed

prop requirements

These are explained in more detail below and a full listing of icons is located on page 16.

Age Group Each game indicates the age group for which it is intended. This means that the game is suitable for or adaptable to children from that age and upward. Feel free to adapt each assignment if you want to use the game for different age groups than those indicated.

Duration The number of minutes indicated is generally the minimum playing time necessary. It is also possible to take certain elements out of a drama game and combine them with another game—which will have other consequences for the program.

The Space Unless otherwise indicated a regular-size classroom is adequate space. The same applies to scenery or other decorations. If the drama game requires special sets or scenery, those suggestions are included with the game.

Players Unless otherwise indicated all of the drama games are suitable for any group of any size. With most games it is useful to divide the players into smaller groups. Each game includes suggestions.

Props Some of the drama games require props, scenery, costumes, or a sound or light installation.

Preparing for a Drama Game

When preparing for a drama game, ask yourself the following questions:

- What is my starting point?
- Who are the players?
- What do I want to achieve?
- Which drama games are suitable for my goals?
- Do I need extra material (sound system, props, costumes, scenery)?
- How will I convey the ideas to the group?
- How will I organize the session so that everyone understands the game?

Be clear about what you want to demonstrate and teach. Change your language or subject matter if necessary. Prepare similar drama games in case you can't use the original game—anything can go wrong with a game, just as it can in the preparation. For example, the size of the group could alter suddenly or the space you want could be unavailable. Be prepared for unexpected changes—and always have an alternative plan.

The Work Space   It is important to prepare the space you will be using for the drama games. The space should invite people to play and should meet the following conditions:

- *Safety*: Make sure the space is clean and free of debris. Are there any sharp objects in the room that could hurt the players?

- *Acoustics:* Can the players hear each other and can they all hear you?

- *Lighting:* Is the lighting adequate? Are a few spotlights needed?

- *Ventilation:* Is it possible to air out the room? Is the room temperature comfortable?

- *Noise:* Is there a chance that the players will disturb other people? Will other people disturb the group's concentration during silent games?

- *Floor covering:* Any flooring that is noisy when walked on will disturb the course of a game. The flooring's material or its covering may also affect a game.

Time and Place Although you can play all day long, let the players determine whether the time and space allotted to the session are satisfactory. The time and duration of a game may depend on the players' age group. For example, children concentrate on games better in the morning.

The Atmosphere Taking part in a game is a voluntary activity; you can't force anyone into it. Try to create a relaxed, inviting atmosphere that will keep the players at ease. Some players may have a resistance to a certain activity. It helps to have a good rapport with the players. This can often prevent a situation where a person does not want to join in. If a person doesn't participate, decide how that will affect the group. For a group just beginning to work together, one person sitting out could be a problem for the others.

Before each game, agree that players won't make negative comments about the way others perform their assignments. Negative criticism not only has a detrimental effect on the atmosphere, but also may make others afraid of expressing themselves freely.

Elements of a Drama Game

During a game, players investigate behavior and use their imaginations. To get through this process, each drama game consists of four elements.

The Introduction In the first phase of the session, players free themselves from daily reality and tune in to the atmosphere of the game (or games) they will be playing. Sensory games are particularly well suited for waking up the class and developing concentration so that the principal game comes across correctly. Another purpose of the warming-up phase is to prepare or explain the parts of the main game.

The Core In this phase, you describe the game's plan. At this point, the purpose of the session becomes clear to the players. For example, the group may have to work together in a particular way, work on a particular form of concentration, or work on the physical planning of a game.

The Process In this phase, you create the climax of the session. At this point the players may share their experiences in short prepared pieces, in a final game devised together, or simply in a serious discussion. Take note of the players' remarks and, if it seems useful, develop a new game for the following meeting or find another suitable game from this book. In this phase, you will find out whether or not you've reached your goals for a particular session. When setting up a complete program, find games that support your goal and direct the session toward it.

Evaluation Following a play session, take time to evaluate what happened and take notes that will help you prepare for subsequent sessions. Use the following questions as guides:

- Was this drama game suitable for these players?

- Did the game fit with their own life experiences?

- Were the assignments well formulated and expressed?

- Was the group sufficiently caught up in the game and was the stimulation well distributed?

- Was the goal for this particular session reached?

- Are there signs of individual or group development?

Sample Game: Promoting Cooperation

Two new members join an already established group. You decide that the goal of the next session will be to promote cooperation between all the group members.

At the beginning of class, introduce one or two sensory games in which the players work together and discover something about each other.

In the core period, introduce a game using props in which players must agree with each other how to use the props. Inspire them to discover different ways to use the objects and emphasize the game's how, why, where, and when aspects (see the section on story games for examples).

In the last phase, divide the players into small groups and have each group create another game that incorporates the aspects already enacted. The small groups demonstrate these to the others. After the session, evaluate whether cooperation within the group has changed.

From Idea to Story Line

You and your group can easily develop a drama game into a production or performance that is much larger than the short pieces the players show each other at the end of a session.

The first step to creating a larger production is developing a theme. To do this, try these brainstorming steps:

- Encourage the players to talk about themes or subjects that interest them.

- On large sheets of paper, take brief notes of everything players express.

- With the players, look through the notes and find one or two themes that the group could use in a large production.

In every story or theme there has to be a conflict, otherwise too little will happen—the buildup of tension is an essential part of an interesting story. There must always be a dramatic situation which allows things to happen. From this you can create a story line, which the audience discovers as they watch the performance. As you create the story line, keep in mind what the audience wants to discover:

- Who is the piece about?

- Where does the story take place?

- When does the story take place?

- How do the leading players behave toward each other?

- What is going to happen to the players?

Once your group has decided on a theme and a story line, the creation of characters takes place naturally. As the players create characters, have them write down the main and supporting roles. Describe the characters, including what they look like; how old they are; if they are men, women, or children;

their relationships with other characters. Just as you know from your own life what kinds of relationships you have, and who your friends are and why, let the players describe their characters in the same way. Collect the information on large sheets of paper so everyone can decide together whether certain roles should be added or deleted.

The Story   A story consists of five parts:

- the introduction
- the approach to the actual story
- the plot
- the approach toward the resolution
- the conclusion

In the *introduction* the audience discovers how the main characters live and act in various situations. They also discover which characters work against each other and any possible problems.

In the *approach* toward the main section an apparently insoluble problem is presented in a familiar situation. Something occurs that sends the story in a new direction.

In the *main section*, the plot, the protagonists and antagonists in the struggle emerge. The good guys and the bad guys do battle, which leads to a climax in which the *final approach* signals the *conclusion*. Something happens that finally turns the story toward a good or bad outcome. It does not have to be a happy ending; it is possible that the problem simply cannot be solved.

You and the players can adapt this story structure to any theme or subject. The important thing is that you know how the story ends and how the conflict in your theme is developed and presented—you have to know in advance how you will bring the game to a close. Consider using a narrator, a song, or a change of scenery in hard-to-act sections of the presentation. The important thing is that you don't attempt to do everything. Let all players get involved; distribute the tasks of lighting, sound, and scenery so that everyone shares in the creation.

Sample Production: Discovery

Take, for instance, the theme of discovery. You can take this theme in any direction you choose, so discuss with the group all the different things the theme suggests to them. Perhaps the following story line emerges.

In scene one, a professor—absent-minded, small, smart, kind to animals—explores a far-off part of the world.

In scene two, the last member of a forgotten species in the forest appears. It is a reindeer that seems alone, sad, and hungry.

In scene three, the professor discovers the animal and decides to record it on film. He also decides to take the reindeer home with him. The journey home is fraught with dangers and setbacks. A hunter who has been searching for years for this reindeer pursues them.

In scene four, the professor arrives home with the reindeer. But the animal is not domesticated and, however hard the professor tries, his whole house becomes a manure heap.

This story has an introduction which features people and an animal, a discovery, a transition to the main story, a series of misadventures that sour the discovery, and then a conclusion in which the professor decides to live in a reindeer shed with his new friend.

As we have already said, you can get a long way by asking the participants the right questions: who are the main characters, when and where does the action take place, how and by what means is the problem solved, and why do you want to present the story in this particular form (what are you trying to say)?

Key to the Icons Used in the Games

Age

Young children (6 and up)

Older children (9 and up)

Teenagers (12 and up)

Time

0 to 10 minutes

10 to 20 minutes

20 to 30 minutes

30 to 60 minutes

60 minutes or more

2 sessions

Props

Props needed
If no icon is shown, no props are needed.

Let's Act: Introductory Games

These games help to put people at ease in a group when they don't know each other very well. The games also provide a chance to discover interesting and special things about other group members.

For many of the introductory games, players work on their assignments independently. The assignments don't take long and progress quickly from one game to another. Within each game, partners change frequently so members get to know everyone and don't have to work with any one partner for too long. Throughout these games, members are concerned with first impressions, "breaking the ice," and becoming acquainted. As you work with a new group, watch carefully to see that all group members feel secure and are encouraged to express themselves.

The Name Game

Invite everyone to sit or stand in a circle with you. Say your first name out loud. Beginning with the group member on your right, have each person say her first name out loud.

Once everyone has called out her name, a new round begins. This time you say the name of the person to your right. Have each player in turn give the name of the person on the right until the circle has been completed.

Who was attentive in the first round and could name the person next to her?

Variations:

- Repeat the game, but this time start with the person on your left.

- When you call out your own name, use some variation in how you say it (for example, loudly, harshly, screaming, a whisper). Other group members may imitate your sound or put their own emotion into it, which will certainly happen unconsciously.

- When you call out your own name, make a movement that expresses how you feel. As in the previous variation, others might imitate your movement or make their own. The strength of the voice and the movement can communicate a lot about the person.

Greetings

Provide two words of greeting ("hello" and "bye," for example). Have the players walk around the room and greet each other with the first word and one person's name, and reply with the second word and the other's name. For example, "Hello, Tim"; "Bye, Sally." If members like, they can also shake hands.

Variations:

- Use the same greeting and add a movement to it, such as a bow when members meet and a wave as they leave. If the group is not yet ready to think of appropriate gestures, suggest two appropriate movements that all players can use.

- Try singing the greetings instead of speaking them. Encourage players to use their own style, from an operatic voice to a rap style.

What Did You Do When You...?

Introduce this game by asking, "Did I tell you what happened when I got up this morning?" Then recount in a couple of sentences what you did. To pass along the story, ask the person next to you, "What did *you* do when you got up this morning?" Once that person has said a few lines, she asks the question of the next person, and so on throughout the group.

Here are some other examples that could challenge group members to create quick answers (prepare these ahead of time so you don't run out of suggestions):

What did you do when...

- "you landed on the moon in your newly built space shuttle?"

- "your teacher suddenly vanished before your eyes?"

- "your pet started talking to you?"

- "you were caught cheating during a test?"

4

Group
Photo

Divide the group into groups of about three to four members each. Suggest a situation to each group and ask the members to take a pose and hold it. Walk around the room and pretend to take a photo of each group. Change the subject of the poses frequently so players don't have too long to think about the poses.

Some examples of situations:

- being outside on a warm summer day

- being outside on a cold winter day—and everyone forgot their coats

- posing as fashion models for a clothing ad

- sitting on a bench and feeding the birds in a park

Variation: Ask each player to bring in group photos of their families or photos from magazines or newspapers that they find interesting. Ask each small group to rehearse four poses. (If the group is not experienced with this type of activity, use a photo as an example and imitate the poses so members can see what they should do.) At the end of the session, ask members to show the original photos and explain what they found interesting about them.

The
Crazy Story

Before the class, find a short story of 10 to 15 sentences and make a copy for each player. Form groups of three to four and have each group member silently read the story. Once everyone has read the story, suggest a different way of telling the story to each group, for example: fearfully, nervously, exuberantly, with relief, like a commercial, like a news report, as a birth announcement, and so on. Encourage group members to convey the message through the way they stand and how they use their voices when telling the story. They don't need to memorize the text.

Variation: For younger players (aged 6 and older), use a rhyme or song that the group knows. Demonstrate different ways of speaking the rhyme or song and ask the group to imitate your actions.

6

Who Are You Now?

Ask group members to walk around the room and greet each other (using phrases like "Hello, how are you?" . . . "Very well, thank you.") according to the suggestions you will give. For example, ask members to greet each other as if they hadn't seen one another in a long time.

Other suggestions include greeting members as if they were your best friends, as if they were your worst enemy, evasively, very shyly, with contempt, or like a robot.

Variations:

- Accompany the greeting with extra gestures, such as hugs when greeting your best friend or turning away when meeting your enemy. Make sure that members avoid aggressive gestures, particularly when meeting their enemies.

- Divide the group into pairs who greet each other as couples.

- Vary the speed and volume of the greetings.

Quick Actions

7

Have the players take a place in the room where they can see everyone else. Perform a short mime, such as brushing your teeth. Ask the group to copy your mime and then quickly point to another player. This player performs another simple mime, the group copies it, the player points to someone else, and so on through the group.

Encourage the players to create the mimes quickly. A few examples are sleepwalking, serving a meal, washing a car, playing tennis, arranging flowers in a vase, and catching a bus.

Variations:

- Instead of copying each other, have each player repeat the movement in their own way. Group members will see a

simple action such as brushing teeth mimed in many different ways—and get to know each other better in the process.

- With a group accustomed to drama games, ask members to accompany their actions with suitable sounds.

- With an experienced group, ask members to create a follow-up action to the one just performed. For example, after brushing your teeth, the next person could mime a logical next step (getting dressed) or an extension of the original action (spitting out the toothpaste).

- Ask the next player to take over the action and extend it. For example, brushing the teeth is extended to the entire body and becomes body-brushing. Encourage players to make absurd caricatures of the original action.

Patterns

Have players mingle as they move around the room. At your signal, ask them to stop and look at the group member you will point to. This person moves in a special way across the room (such as swaying to and fro in sweeping steps, using angular movements, swirling in circles, and so on). All the other players copy the pattern. After everyone has repeated the pattern, point to another member who starts a new movement.

If necessary, demonstrate a couple of movements. Ask players to think about what kind of movement suits them best.

Variations:

- If someone likes the pattern another player made, she can repeat it and doesn't have to change movements. In this way small groups will form and meet up as they move around the room with their own individual patterns. Watch that none of the groups disturbs those players working alone. Ask the group who prefers the angular movements and who the rounded ones.

- Make a sound for each movement and sing the sound during the movement. Have the other players imitate both sound and movement to experience the way in which you move, play, and sing.

- Have each pattern suggest a situation: jumping in crisscross movements through the park, mowing diagonally across a lawn, and so on. Give the pattern some kind of dramatic aspect.

Your Favorite Place

Think of a favorite pleasing or interesting place—such as a castle, forest, zoo, or playground—and pretend to guide the group around it. For example, in a castle show them a secret door, a creaky staircase, and portraits hung in a long hallway. The tour should last no longer than a minute. When the time is up, point to a player and ask her to show the group around her favorite place. When she is done, have her point to another player and so on throughout the group.

The other players should become immediately involved in the story. When the first player stands still and points to another player, the latter should continue with a completely different atmosphere.

Act Your Story

Form a circle and tell the players that they will be contributing to a story that will be created as the game is played. Start by standing in the middle of the circle and acting out the initial few motions of a story then ask a player to switch places with you and continue the story. Each player can decide how much fantasy to add to the story. You might also want the group to agree that once a main character is introduced, that character has to remain in the story.

Variation: The leader begins with the story and passes it on to another player. He introduces the player by name with the question, "And what did Joe (the player's own name) do next?" Each player tries to join in and everyone who takes part portrays something different. As a player performs the story, the others see if they have something to add. When it's time to pass on the story, ask a leading question of the next player.

For example, your story might begin with a biker cycling down a road. When you're done, say to the next player, "There was a strong wind and suddenly the biker lost control of the bike and fell. What happened next?"

Sensory Games

The games in this section help members use their senses and develop their concentration. Good acting requires good perception. Throughout these sensory games, encourage players to observe when others use their senses well and when they don't. They should observe how a person moves and speaks, observe objects and animals, smell different materials, taste different things, feel whether an object is hard or soft. Once your group has tried the whole range of sensory experiences, they can apply their experiences to any role they choose to play.

During these games, make sure players are never put into dangerous situations. Do not offer dangerous or unsafe substances to feel, taste, touch, or smell. Be aware that some players may have allergies to certain materials or foods and use caution when introducing those substances.

11

The
Feeling Story

Before the class, gather materials and objects that players can touch, smell, taste, and hear (for example, a bowl of gelatin, cotton balls, tree bark, raisins, small bells). Arrange the objects around a large room and have towels and bowls of water available for players to rinse their hands, if necessary. Avoid any dirty or dangerous materials.

Pair off the players and let one be the leader and the other be the follower. The leaders blindfold the followers and lead them around the room touching, tasting, smelling, or listening to the sound of the different objects. As the followers experience each object, the leaders make up a story about it. For example, as a follower touches the cotton balls, the leader might talk about flying through the air and feeling fluffy clouds. Then the leader could take the follower to the tree bark and talk about landing in a beautiful forest.

Once the leaders have taken their followers to all the objects around the room and told their stories, they switch places.

12

What Are You Passing On?

Before the class, gather small objects of different shapes and materials (for example, an eraser, a roll of tape, a stuffed animal, a mitten) and place them in a bag.

Ask the group to sit in a circle and have players put on blindfolds. Take an object out of the bag and give it to a person in the circle. Ask that person to describe how the object feels without saying what it is and then hand it to the person sitting next to him. Have each player say something about the object's characteristics (for example, whether it's hard or soft, cold or hot, smooth or rough). Let group members say as much as they can about the object. If necessary, blindfold yourself and give an extensive description of an object as an example. Have the last person in the circle try to guess what the object is without touching it.

Hands
and
Face

Divide the players into two groups and blindfold one group. Ask the players without blindfolds to find a blindfolded player and let that person touch their hands and face. Can the blindfolded person guess who they are feeling? After each blindfolded person has touched two or three different partners, let the groups switch roles.

Touching other people and being blindfolded are not things everyone enjoys. Be aware of this and don't force anyone to join in if they don't feel comfortable. If the players don't know each other, this makes a good introductory game.

A Different Space

Duration: 30 minutes, 10 minutes for preparation

Divide the players into two groups. Have one group put on blindfolds and take the other to another room. Have them alter a familiar room or corridor by changing the position of furniture and objects in that space. When the room is ready, have them lead the blindfolded group through the space. Then let the second group have a chance to rearrange the room and lead the first group through it.

Who Does It Belong To?

This game helps to improve observation skills. Sit the players in a circle and ask them to look at each other for a few minutes. At your signal, have everyone put something of theirs in the center of the circle (for example, a piece of clothing, a shoe, or a piece of jewelry). Ask one person to pick up an article and hand it to the person he thinks it belongs to. One by one everyone picks up an article and returns it to the owner. If the player is wrong, the real owner claims her belonging.

Variations:

- When a player picks up an object from the center of the circle, ask her to say who she thinks it belongs to and why (ensure that each story has a positive focus).

- Once the owner has his object, ask him to tell where he got the article and why he likes or dislikes it. If the object's story is particularly interesting, have the group act it out.

- With the articles in the middle of the circle, have a member describe her object and tell or act a story about it. Can someone in the circle pick out the right article? Can members figure out what it is from the story?

Everything That Is Round

Ask group members to bring in objects that are round. Set up a place in the room to display them. Ask members to talk about the objects they brought and why they are special. What other round objects do they notice in the room or building?

Variations:

- Have members bring in objects of other shapes, such as triangular, diamond-shaped, and square.

- As the players view the display, remove one of the objects. Who can guess which object is missing?

- With the group, arrange the objects by type or size.

- Ask the group which objects suggest a story. (For example, what kind of story could the group make up about a round rock or ring?)

Looking
with
Your Eyes
Closed

Ask group members to sit in a circle and close their eyes. When you tap one of the members on the shoulder, she should describe another member of the group without mentioning his name. She should do this as precisely as she can, talking about what the other person looks like, special physical characteristics, and perhaps a little about his personality (agree in advance to only speak positively about other group members). The others listen carefully; when they think they know who is being described, they may raise their hands. At your signal, everyone opens their eyes and the speaker tells who she was describing.

The group can repeat this game two or three times.

18

I Spy
with
My Little Eye

Ask a group member to describe something in the room. Encourage the person to say as much as possible about the object, but not to mention the color, the shape, nor what it is unless no one can guess correctly.

Variations:

- Place a variety of objects under a sheet in the middle of the circle. Have members close their eyes while one member pulls an object from underneath the sheet and describes it to the group.

- With experienced players, ask members to create a situation involving the object. For example, with a hat, the speaker could describe an article worn by the new kid in school.

19

A Journey Through the Room

Duration: 30 minutes for the game, 30 minutes for preparation

Before the class starts, place objects around the room that make some sort of sound. These could include bells, dry leaves, spoons and pots and pans, or small musical instruments.

Divide the members into pairs and have one of the pair be the leader, the other the follower. The leader blindfolds the follower, then takes the follower to each object in turn and makes up a story as the follower makes a sound with the object. Avoid unpleasant, sudden noises that can startle players. The object of the game is not to create excitement but for the players to experience the different sounds in a receptive environment.

Can You Hear What They're Playing?

Many amateur actors don't speak clearly. As a result, audiences often cannot understand or follow a play. This game can help young actors make the reading of text fun, both to listen to and watch.

Before the class, choose text from a book or magazine that has plenty of dialogue for every player. (As an alternative, write your own scene with speaking parts for many actors.) Give copies to each group member. Divide the class into small groups and ask one group to read through the piece in a normal voice. Then ask a different group to perform the piece by yelling the words; ask another group to perform it in a whisper, or have members change the volume in the middle.

Variations:

- Ask one group to read the piece very softly—to the extent that the listeners can barely hear the players speaking and must watch their lips and their actions to follow the sketch.

- Ask the group to use highly exaggerated actions and tone and perform the piece in slow motion. Have the players start so softly that the words can just be heard, and then gradually increase the volume.

Both variations use a considerable amount of concentration but are fun to do and interesting to listen to.

Bottles of What?

Before class, gather several empty plastic bottles with caps. Fill each bottle with a different material (such as dried peas, pebbles, marbles, sand, and birdseed). Put the caps back on and cover the bottles with construction paper so the materials inside are hidden.

Ask group members to listen to the sound each bottle makes and guess what is inside it.

22

Listening Blind

Divide the group into pairs, with one person being the leader and the other the follower. Have all the followers line up on one side of the room and all the leaders on the other. Blindfold the followers and ask the leaders to guide them across the room using only verbal instructions.

Begin with one leader instructing her follower. Gradually add more leaders guiding their followers. Once the followers have all reached their leaders, have the two groups switch places.

Variation: The game could also be a treasure hunt in which each pair agrees on signals for going in one direction or going high or low.

23

Mystery Box Treats

Suitable for ages 4 and up

A few days before you play this game, give each group member a small box with a lid and ask them to fill it with some sort of snack (for example, bits of cereal, raisins, small crackers, or pretzels).

On the day of the game, display the boxes and let each member taste a sample from each box. Encourage members to talk about what they are tasting.

Variation: Blindfold group members and have them taste the snacks. Ask them how they figure out what the foods are.

24

Taste Everything

In this game, group members bring in their favorite things to eat and share them with other members. Let parents know ahead of time that they'll need to help prepare food. Have extra snacks on hand in case some members forget. You'll need plenty of adult help to serve the food, provide napkins, and clean up.

As members taste the food others have brought, encourage them to describe the tastes, compliment the cooks, and ask questions about how something was prepared. Keep the members talking about the food, including guessing ingredients and suggesting other, complementary foods.

25

Imagining the Taste

This game is about making other people's mouths water. Have each player in turn describe something to eat—encourage members to use as much detail as possible and wildly exaggerate the smells, tastes, and textures of the food.

Then have the group talk about the actual eating of the food (for example, talk about how ice cream melts on your tongue or how peanut butter sticks to the roof of your mouth before swallowing).

Variations:

• Make an outer circle of listeners and an inner circle of speakers. The speakers move along one place at a time and whisper in each listener's ear details about a particular food. Have the listeners keep their eyes closed so that they can better envisage the food.

• Describe a single aspect of a food, for example, the juice of a peach at the peak of its ripeness.

26

I Can't Stand

Have each player in turn describe a food that they cannot stand to eat. Encourage as much detail as possible so that the other group members are disgusted by the food, too.

It Smells Like

Before class, gather several objects that give off a strong odor, such as perfume, spices, cat food, and flowers. Put each in a jar with a lid.

Have the class sit in a circle and close their eyes. Uncover one of the jars and have members take turns smelling what's inside. Ask them to describe what they are smelling, but not to name the object. Once the object has been around the circle, members can open their eyes. Make sure that no dangerous or unsafe substances are used. (If any group members have allergies, they should not take part in this game if there is any risk of them developing a reaction.)

Sniffing

Suitable for ages 4 and up

What does a newly washed woolen sweater smell like? or a freshly peeled hard-boiled egg? or an old mop? If you think they smell like a sweater, egg, or mop, smell again. Many people don't develop their sense of smell or pay attention to what they smell—and that's too bad, because the world is full of scents, some fragrant and others decidedly unpleasant.

A few days before you play this sniffing game, ask each group member to bring in an object with an interesting smell.

Have the group sit in a circle and pass the objects around so that people can look at them and become aware of each object's unique smell. Ask each player to say something about each smell, whether he finds it pleasant or not, and what it reminds him of. Does the smell fit the object?

The Story of Smells

Suitable for ages 4 and up

Before the class meets, gather several objects that give off strong odors and place them in jars with lids, as described in game 27.

During class, make up a story (or have a pair of players make up a story) in which there are many chances to smell the objects in the jars. As the story is being told, pass around the jar with the appropriate object in it. Make sure that the object is passed around the entire group and that the description of it is lengthy, otherwise the story will continue too quickly and some people will not experience listening to the story and smelling the object at the same time.

The Scent

You and the group can play this game either indoors or outdoors. Before the class, create a trail of objects through your building or room that group members must follow by smell. The objects used shouldn't have a very strong or persistent smell, or one that makes people feel sick. For example, the coatroom could smell of flowers, a cupboard could smell of baked potatoes, and a corner of a room could smell like perfume. Once the trail is set, create a map of the route and make a copy for each group member.

Ask members to follow the map and color it in using different colors to indicate the different smells. For example,

suggest members use a darker color crayon for smells they find unpleasant and lighter colors for pleasant smells.

Variation: Organize a walk through a neighborhood or local mall where you know you will encounter certain smells. For example, plan your route so the group walks by a bakery, factory, pet store, or car repair garage.

Pantomime Games

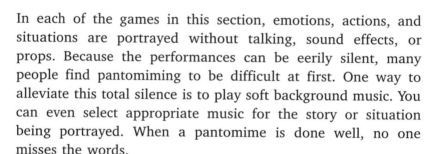

In each of the games in this section, emotions, actions, and situations are portrayed without talking, sound effects, or props. Because the performances can be eerily silent, many people find pantomiming to be difficult at first. One way to alleviate this total silence is to play soft background music. You can even select appropriate music for the story or situation being portrayed. When a pantomime is done well, no one misses the words.

In pantomime, players imitate actions as closely as possible and generally exaggerate. The actions portrayed are drawn out and the movements are enlarged so that the audience can clearly understand the story being told.

Pantomime games can be rehearsed separately and worked out as an independent form of play. They can also serve well as a part (an intermission, for example) of a larger dramatic performance.

The Mystery Object

Suitable for ages 4 and up

This game acts as a preparation for game 32 (The Invisible Object).

Before the class starts, gather several objects with different characteristics; for example, a smooth stone, rough sandpaper, a soft towel, and a cold apple.

Have the players sit on chairs in a circle and pass around one of the objects. Tell each player to hold the object for a moment and really feel it before passing it to the next person. Ask questions about the objects as the players pass them around: How heavy or light is the object? How large or small is it? Does the object have soft or hard edges? When the players have become aware of these properties, pass the objects around again. This time ask the players to close their eyes and imagine the object's characteristics.

Variation: Pass around an object covered in such a way that players can't tell what it is. (For example, wrap several thick towels around a large rock.) Accentuate the effect by passing around an object that moves or is pliable, such as a piece of dough wrapped in a sheet or water sealed in a plastic bag.

The Invisible Object

Play this game after group members have completed game 31 (The Mystery Object).

Have the group sit on chairs in a circle and "give" one player an invisible object. Encourage members to hold, examine, and pass along the object. Make sure the invisible object retains its original shape and size.

Ask questions about the invisible object as players pass it around the circle: Did the object change in the hands of the previous player? Has it become a different object? Was it clear what kind of object it was?

Variations:

- When you hand the invisible object to the first player, tell him what it is (for example, a pan, a fish, or a bowling ball).

- Handling invisible moving and pliable objects is difficult and requires special practice. An invisible fish that slides out of one's hands invites clowning around; it's fun to see how players deal with this situation.

- As it is passed around, the player handling the invisible object says what it is. The following player remolds the object with her hands. She then says what the new object is.

Is It a Teapot?

Ask players to create an object independently or in small groups and practice transforming it four or five times. For example, you can hit a cue ball with an invisible billiard stick; which then becomes a walking cane or flagpole. The transformations don't need to be logical; encourage players to transform all sorts of objects together.

During the thinking and practice period, walk around the room and provide inspiration where necessary. Assemble the group and have players demonstrate in a slow sequence what they have rehearsed. The spectators try to identify each object in turn.

The Imaginary Room

You and the group can play this game by itself or, for quicker results, immediately after games 31, 32, and 33 (The Mystery Object, The Invisible Object, and Is It a Teapot?).

Divide the players into groups of four and tell each group to create its own imaginary room. Without saying a word or making a sound, demonstrate your room as an example: switch on a light, find a cup in a cupboard and pour a glass of milk, make sure no one bumps into one of your chairs. Once players understand the assignment, provide some time for them to rehearse. Encourage members to fill their rooms with furniture, light switches, and windows—anything they can think of.

Assemble the players and have each group show its room to the others—remind them that there is to be no talking or making sounds.

Variations:

- Ask each small group to create an event in the room. For example, someone faints and lies on the ground or the TV doesn't work when you turn it on.

- Create a story for each small group in which an object is missing; ask the members to portray the problem. For example, friends are coming over to eat and there aren't enough chairs or the group wants to drive a car but the keys are missing.

35

Sports Doubles

Miming a sport such as football appears simple, but it's not just a matter of being familiar with the sport. Mimes must also have strong observation skills to act out all the actions involved in a particular sport.

Divide the group into pairs and have each one pick a sport to mime. As part of the sport, have each pair also mime an event. For example, one volleyball player hits the ball so hard that it deflates; two basketball players bump into each other; a table-tennis ball gets stuck in the net. Make sure that the players emphasize the actions which belong to their sport. Not a single movement should be made gratuitously.

Give each pair a minute to rehearse and then have each demonstrate their sporting adventure to the others. The performances should not last more than a minute.

Talking with Your Body

Children make all sorts of movements—they put their hands in front of their face to tease someone; they use their hands as barriers for toy cars. In this game players pretend they suddenly can't talk and need to rely on hand gestures to convey something to the group.

Divide the players into small groups and ask each one to create four actions. For example, portray anger by wildly swinging arms or sadness by slumping over. Walk around the room during rehearsals and make suggestions where necessary.

37

Pass on a Message

Before the class, write several simple messages on small pieces of paper. Some examples are "It's cold outside," "I have a sandwich for lunch," and "I like to ride my bike."

Have the group sit in a circle and communicate one of the messages to the first player, using only gestures. This player passes on the message as she understands it, using only gestures, to the next player. Stop the game at a certain point and ask the player whose turn it is if she can explain the message without enacting it. Read the original message to the group. Has the message been passed on correctly? How is it different or similar to the original message?

Variations:

- When you enact the message for the first player, tell him what it is. That player then adds to the message using only gestures. The message with the added gestures keeps going around the room with every player adding something. For example, for the original message "Do you want to cook the potatoes first or slice the vegetables," a player could add a gesture showing he's cutting the vegetables and cuts his finger or cuts too many vegetables and overfills the pot.

- Divide the group into pairs and communicate using only gestures. In another conversation, have one of the members speak while the other communicates with gestures.

Is That a Job?

Have the group sit in a circle and watch while you mime an occupation (such as a mail carrier, firefighter, nurse, or ticket taker). Let each player have a chance to mime an occupation.

In the second round, ask group members to mime an occupation that either doesn't exist or is imaginary (such as an umbrella repair person, felt-tip pen filler, town crier, or motorcycle school principal).

Variation: Let small groups of players enact an occupation. Have the group agree in advance which role each member will play. Encourage the groups to think of a job where the assistants can caricature their roles during the performance. Repetitions of the actions can often be comical and supportive for the main actor.

The Saying

Together with the group, think of several sayings or slang expressions that members use or know about, such as "That's cool" or "Put a lid on it." Then act out the literal meaning of the words—not the slang meaning. You can also mime such expressions as "She let the cat out of the bag" or "He spilled the beans."

Variations:

- Once the group has acted out several sayings and expressions, alter the sayings and act them out again. For example, "I'll do whatever you say" could become "I'll do whatever you say not to do."

- Mime is generally performed without props. You may, however, choose to present the sayings with the help of props. The words "I" and "you" in the variation above could be written on cards.

A Tale Without Sound

When performing a story without sound, each player has to know exactly which actions he or she will perform in order to enact the story with natural exaggeration.

With the players, pick a well-known story and decide the number of scenes. For example, for "Little Red Riding Hood" the scenes may be the following: Mother talks with Red Riding Hood, the wolf walks through the forest, Red Riding Hood sets off through the forest, the wolf arrives at Grandma's house, Red Riding Hood talks to the disguised wolf, and so on. Now ask the players to translate the scenes into movements. If this is too difficult for an inexperienced class, let smaller groups act out the same tale as a practice round.

Variation: Act out a story without words but use appropriate sounds (in Red Riding Hood, for example, use howling or sniffing sounds for the wolf). Each group can choose what sounds they think will be fun and important enough for the performance. The extra sounds add a strange but engaging element to the action.

41

Trans-
formations

In preparation for this game, play game 32 (The Invisible Object) first, unless the group already has enough experience in miming actions.

Ask everyone to sit in a circle. Present an invisible object to one of the players who immediately transforms it out of proportion, making it extremely small or extremely large. For example, a player could turn a straw into one that is so huge and ridiculously heavy that she needs other players to help support it. Let the straw pass from player to player, taking on so many new dimensions that it no longer resembles a straw. The next player in the circle passes along a new invisible object. Can others guess what the object is after it is transformed?

The Same Situation Twice

In this game, small groups act out the same situation twice: once as it should turn out and once as the group members want it to turn out.

Divide the players into several groups and ask them to act out lifting up a couch and moving it to another position. Then give the groups a few minutes to decide a different outcome to the lifting and moving of the couch. For example, someone could get stuck between the sofa and the door or get hit by the sofa when the player holding the other end is distracted. With experienced players, encourage more complicated outcomes to the same situation.

Slow-Motion Movie

For this game, players act out a scene from a movie. Before the class, choose a movie scene that shows an event and an actor (or actors) reacting to the event (such as someone getting hit in the face with a pie). Choose a scene that shows the actor's whole body.

At the beginning of the class, let the players view the scene. Tell them that this scene is made up of a number of different shots and images that have been put together to form the action of the scene (some scenes include twenty images). Divide the players into small groups and ask them to perform the same scene in slow motion (as slow as possible), as if they are playing back the movie at the wrong speed. Give each group time to rehearse.

Variations:

- Show several subsequent scenes from the same movie and assign a different scene to each group. Have the groups perform the scenes in order.

- Accompany the acting with appropriate sounds, which are slowed down. Although the audience won't be able to actually understand a conversation, it is great fun to portray the dragged-out stream of sound.

Funny Faces Show

Props: video camera or a regular camera (preferably one that provides instant photos)

Before the class, write down different emotions (such as fear, happiness, worry, excitement, concern, and dismay) on small pieces of paper. Be sure that there are enough for each player to choose five.

At the beginning of class, have each player choose their five emotions. Then give them a few minutes to think about the facial expressions they will use to convey the emotions. You might show a slapstick film to give the class ideas about using different facial expressions to convey emotions. You could also take a theme or story as a starting point.

As each player runs through her facial expressions, record or photograph them. Once everyone has had a chance to show their expressions, play back the video or pass around the instant photographs and see if the group can guess the emotions being portrayed.

Variations:

- If no camera is available, divide the class into pairs, with one member acting as a mirror to the other. Have the pairs rehearse together and then show the group their expressions and imitations.

- Ask players to make suitable sounds with each expression. With pairs, have the partner comment on the expression; she could give the funny face a title or explain the situation in a few words.

- Divide the group into pairs and ask each pair to enact an existing fairy tale or story through facial expressions. One member can be the narrator, explaining the story behind the funny expression, while the other player holds the expression for a moment for the rest of the group to see.

The Game of the Doors

One action often neglected in mime is the opening and closing of doors. But without this action, many scenes couldn't even begin. There are always moments of entry and departure, and every door is different—some revolve, some are heavy or bolted, some squeak or swing.

Divide the players into small groups and ask each group to create and rehearse a situation in which doors are important. Then have the groups act out the scene for the whole group. Ensure that small actions (such as putting a key in a lock) are slightly enlarged and enacted slowly and clearly. Enter the game through a door or a series of doors. This way the players will be involved right away.

Just as in other games, a story may serve as inspiration, but the group's experience with improvisation determines whether this is necessary. Give the game closure by having everyone leave through an imaginary door.

Walk-On Game

A walk-on is someone who takes part in a drama and adds to the action through his or her fairly unobtrusive presence. This might mean, for example, that an actor appears in a grocery store scene but does not have a speaking part. He or she simply plays the role of a customer as naturally as possible. The main actors play the chief characters and speak the lines.

Divide the players into small groups. Ask each group to create a situation in which one player speaks the lines and the others perform actions (repeating them as necessary) in order to set the atmosphere and create a natural scenario. Give the groups time to rehearse and then have each perform their piece for the rest of the class.

After each scene, talk about the way the situation was played out and other options the players could have chosen.

Story Games

The games in this section explain the elements of a story and how to put them together to act out its different parts.

All stories have a beginning, a middle, and an end. The beginning, or introduction, explains who the story is about, the situation in which the character lives or works, and what problems arise. After the introduction comes a transition by which the story line suddenly changes direction and the story itself begins to develop. The character encounters problems that he must resolve. At the end of this central section comes the long-awaited transition to the solution: the conclusion.

In this series of games, players have plenty of practice developing and acting story beginnings, transitions, and endings. As they learn more about each story's parts, they will be able to apply this knowledge to stories that they create.

47

Creating Characters

Props: dress-up clothes, if available

To create and act out a story, actors need to know what the story is about and who is involved. Before the class, write down several questions group members should consider when creating a character for a story. Some sample questions include:

- What are the main character's distinguishable traits (for example, age, name, young or old, male or female, rich or poor)?

- Where does the main character live?

- What is the character's history (for example, where was the person born; where does the person work; does the person have children/brothers or sisters/parents)?

- What is the situation in which the character currently finds himself or herself?

Divide the players into small groups and give each group a copy of the prepared questions. Give the groups fifteen minutes to develop characters and rehearse their actions. If props or costumes are available, let the groups use them. As a group acts out the characteristics of its characters, the rest of the class can ask questions about them. While staying in character, players answer the questions.

The first time a group tries this game, players may feel a bit awkward. After creating characters in this way once or twice, however, the preparation will be easier and completed more quickly.

One Hundred Stories

Props: pens and index cards (four cards for each player)

This game is a sequel to game 47 (Creating Characters).

Give each player a pen and four index cards. Ask them to create four different characters and write a little about each on an index card. Some character ideas are a doctor, jeweler, bandit, little girl, elderly man, or grade school kid. When the players have created their characters, gather all the index cards and put them in a pile.

Divide the players into groups of four and have each member pick four index cards from the pile. Give them some time to make up a short play using their four characters. Encourage group members to talk about how the characters might interact with one another. What kinds of problems will the four characters have to solve?

49

The First and Last Sentences

This game is a sequel to game 48 (One Hundred Stories). It gives players practice in fleshing out a story between a given beginning and ending. When creating a story or play, it is useful to know how it will end. Once you know what you are working toward, you can think of a good beginning.

Before class, write down several story beginnings each one on a separate index card. Then write several story endings. Make sure there are varied types of situations so players can fantasize about the atmosphere and content. Some possible beginnings include: On a bright winter morning, the family hears a knock on their front door; On the first day of June, the science class decides to explore the nearby woods. Some possible endings include: And no one bothered the troll ever again; And that's how the neighborhood kids saved the town.

Divide the players into small groups and ask each group to pick a beginning and an ending sentence. Have each make up a play that begins and ends with the sentences on their two cards—nothing can be said or acted before the first or after the last sentence.

Variation: Once players are accustomed to creating stories using a given beginning and ending, prepare cards that give only a last sentence, showing how a story ends. If necessary, explain the sentences on the cards.

An Exciting Beginning

This game is a follow-up to game 49 (The First and Last Sentences).

Every story needs an opening that immediately captures the attention of audience members—otherwise they won't be interested in the rest of the story. In this game, small groups act out only the beginning of a story and the audience has to guess how it will turn out. The group members, however, have already decided how the story ends.

Divide players into small groups and ask each group to create a main character, a plot (including an ending), a situation for the characters at the story's beginning, and a title. Give each group ten minutes to think of and rehearse an exciting opening before performing it for the rest of the class. The performance of each opening should not last longer than a few minutes.

Tableau Transitions

Play this game in connection with games 47, 48, 49, and 50.

This game gives players a deeper understanding of what goes into setting up a story line and enacting a play. It is concerned with transitions: just when the audience thinks they know what a story is about, the story line suddenly changes direction—something happens or a problem arises that influences events and steers the story in a different way.

In this game, players use text and movements in combination with tableaux (freezing the action and text at a typical moment of the situation). In a tableau, the players all freeze in

fixed positions at the same moment, and the audience sees what is happening as a living, but still life, painting.

Divide the players into small groups and present each with the same beginning to a story. Let each group rehearse and then demonstrate their interpretation of the beginning using a series of tableaux. Encourage players to perform the transition from one scene to another gradually and in slow motion so that audience members can see the situation changing.

When players are familiar with thinking in images to interpret a new situation, ask them to perform the transitions that follow the introduction until the conclusion. Each short play should last approximately five minutes.

52

Yet More Problems

As other games in this section have shown, it helps actors to know a story's ending before they enact the beginning. Actors also need to know a story's sudden transitions or changes. Then they can develop the middle section (including problems to be solved) that leads to the ending.

Before class, create several stories that small groups can enact and write the titles of the stories on index cards. For each story, include information about the main character, what happened at the story's beginning, and what the main character may expect. You could also include the ending.

Divide the players into small groups and have each one choose an index card. Ask each group to create several problems that could occur in the story's middle section. Allow time to rehearse and then let each group perform their middle sections for the entire class.

The Serial Story

Preparation: half a day; rehearsal and performance— 2 hours for each part of the story

A serial story is one that is broken into parts, such as one that was originally designed for newspapers (a different part of the story would appear each week until its ending). For this game, the serial story will:

- Start with an opening tune, a short, recognizable melody that opens each part of the story.

- Include a recapitulation (summing up what happened to the characters last time).

- Continue the story, which players may embellish with short musical interludes.

- End with a recapitulation before, during, or after the theme tune.

Explain the idea of the serial story to the players and brainstorm ideas for a story line, including the ultimate situation and ending. Create a main character and supporting roles, a theme, and a time and place for the story's action. Once the story is complete, decide how many episodes the group will need to tell the story (each episode should take no more than 10 to 15 minutes).

With the players, decide who will take care of the music, scenery, scene changes, costumes, and who will play each character.

Sound Games

For some people, it's difficult to imagine a world without sound; others take everyday noises and sounds for granted. The games in this section make players more aware of the sounds around them. The games become more interesting as more players use sound and sound effects. In each game, an appropriate use of the human voice is of vital importance. The extra sounds made in these games draw players' attention to the close connections among sound, the voice, and the play itself.

The Right Sounds

In a play characters usually use dialogue and gestures—not sound effects—to show action. Even if a character enters a scene with great commotion, the sound of the door swinging open is not emphasized. In this game, however, sounds such as this are amplified.

Divide the players into groups and ask each one to create a short story lasting two or three minutes. Explain that the story should contain extra sound effects. Encourage them to exaggerate every action in a situation by putting extra emphasis on the sounds. This could mean that a squeaky door squeaks a little longer and footsteps are louder and stronger. Give each group time to rehearse and then have them act out their story with sound effects for the rest of the class.

Variations:

- You can strengthen the extra sound effects by using a microphone or extra players. The extra players can make the sounds from the side of the stage instead of the actors themselves making them. These extra players have to make the right sounds at the right moment and at the right volume. Group members might use a director to indicate when to make the sound effects. The director can tell these extra players when to add footstep noises and how long they should last.

- Ask the players to make all the sound effects using only their voices. You could also limit the groups to a few items that produce sounds. You might wish to begin by working with the group to discover sounds using various objects: for example, how could you make the sound of an approaching train using tin cans?

- Repeat certain sound effects and adapt the game accordingly. For example, a character entering the room could open and close the door several times because he keeps remembering things he forgot to bring in from the car. The sound effects will become more and more prominent.

The Wrong Sounds

This game is similar to game 54 (The Right Sounds), except that now the players create sounds that *don't* match the action. When a character opens a door, for example, a bell rings. Through the use of different sounds, players can add humor to a play.

Divide the players into small groups and ask each to create a short play (no more than a few minutes in length) in which the accompanying sounds don't fit the action at all. Encourage the groups to vary the number, strength, and volume of each sound. This might mean that walking is accompanied by a variety of sound effects: shoes clomping along with the action or coconut shells making sounds like horses' hooves. Remind the groups to keep the story in mind and not to totally negate the plot with their sound effects.

High and Low

Everyone makes verbal slips from time to time. Sometimes you mispronounce a word, or you mean one thing but say another; your voice suddenly gets higher, lower, or hoarse; you put the accent on the wrong part of a word. In this game, players deliberately make their voices high or low at the wrong moments.

Divide the players into small groups and pick a well-known story or have the groups make up their own stories. Encourage them to exaggerate the pitch of their voices while they act out the story—but at the same time, tell them to try to enact the situation as clearly as possible.

The News

Props: (optional) microphones and a sound system

Divide the players into pairs. Explain that each pair will create its own newscast, including local news, the weather for tomorrow and the rest of the week, and coming events for the players' school or club. As an added twist, each news reporter must use a voice different from her own. Players could read the news in an extra high voice or an extra low one, rapidly, slowly, in a monotone, or exaggerating every word.

Each newscast should last several minutes. Although microphones and speakers are not essential to this game, they add to the possibilities for playing with the voices.

Cheer-leaders

In this game, players prepare to be an audience. Sitting in a circle, lead the group in practicing audience sound effects. Some examples are applause, cheering, booing, loudly eating potato chips, crumpling paper, empathizing with the actors, crying and laughing, coughing and sneezing, and so on. The idea is for the players to make these sounds using their own voices and hands or some props if they need them.

Now arrange the group as an audience watching an imaginary show. They can do this in different positions and for different kinds of events: a TV talk show or sitcom, a basketball or football game, a play rehearsal or a parade, a terrible movie or a long church sermon.

Variation: The leader can ask for the participation of this 'public' in a subsequent class.

Guessing Game

Props: tape player and blank tapes

Divide the players into small groups. Ask each group to create a short play that includes many sounds (for example, a birthday party, a visit to a zoo, or cooking and preparing a feast). The play shouldn't last more than a few minutes and should have more sound effects than dialogue.

When the groups have created their plays, ask each in turn to leave the room and record its story and sound effects. Later, all the players can listen to the tapes and guess what each play is about.

60

Words with Sounds

Props: pen and paper for each player

Divide the players into small groups. Before they break into their groups, however, have everyone sit in a circle with their own pen and paper. Call out a word and imitate its sound, and ask the players to write down ten words associated with that sound. For example, you could say "sea" and make the sound of crashing waves. The players might write down *loud, cold, wet, foamy, frightening, watery, bubbly, soaking, dripping*, and *damp*. Call out enough words and sounds so that each small group will have a word to work with.

Let the players break into their groups and assign one word to each group. Ask each group to create a play in which they interpret their word in sound. For example, players in the group that has the word "sea" would use *loud, cold, wet, foamy*, and other words that their members thought of. Encourage groups to choose some players who will act and other players who will create the sound effects. After about ten minutes of rehearsal, have the players perform their play for the rest of the class.

Interference Game

Divide the players into small groups and ask each to create a short improvisation about anything they want. Give each group a few minutes to rehearse. Now ask each group to think of some noises (of all types of volumes) that they can use to disrupt another group's performance.

Ask the first group to perform their improvisations. Tell the rest of the class to watch carefully to see where they could add surprising sound effects. Ask the group to perform their improvisation again, and this time invite the rest of the class to inject sound effects whenever and wherever they want.

Make sure each group gets to both perform and to interfere with a performance. The group performing should try to continue the performance despite the interference.

62

Twins

Divide the players into pairs and tell the members of the pairs they are connected to each other by an imaginary thread. Ask each pair to tell a complete story in ten to fifteen sentences. The tricky part is that they must alternate sentences; the first player says something and her partner enhances it. Provide a story subject for the pair and let them improvise the story for the other players.

Variation: Suggest that all the pairs use the exact same words to convey a story. Allow some rehearsal time before each pair recites its story for the group.

63

You Get Too Nervous

Before class, choose a short story or scenario that is familiar to everyone in the group. The story should have both dialogue and action.

Divide the players into small groups and ask each group to perform the story in a different way: as if they were nervous or angry; softly and shyly; with long pauses; without taking a breath (as few pauses as possible); screaming the words, or singing them.

Games with Props

Props are aids that players sometimes need when performing a play. With the help of props, an actor can create an atmosphere more directly and clearly than through words and gestures alone. An actor may need just one prop for a play, or a large number of the same object in order to get an idea across to the audience. For example, with a hundred balloons an actor can create a festive feeling, or releasing one helium balloon could symbolically illustrate a farewell.

64

A Broomstick Is a Horse

Props: everyday objects such as brooms, buckets, chairs, blankets, small tables, or stools

You can transform any space by using available materials and objects. If you know what a play is about, you can look for objects that fit the situation.

Before class begins, gather several everyday objects. Divide the players into groups of four and ask them to create a short play using no more than four of the objects. Also instruct players to imagine unusual uses for each object; they can't use a broom for sweeping or a chair for sitting.

The Fashion Show

Duration: a whole morning or afternoon; planning: 2 hours

Props: spotlights; a backdrop; a raised platform or catwalk, if possible; a sound system

Putting on a fashion show can be fun for all players, especially if everyone gets to choose the role they will play. In the planning stages, let the players decide on a theme for the show (such as fall fashions, holiday outfits, or beachwear), suitable music, and which role to play—model (male or female), designer,

emcee, journalist, photographer. Help the players plan the stage setup, mark where people will enter and exit and where the audience will sit. Make a list of special clothes people will wear during the show and any other props the show might need.

At the second session, give members time to set up the show and get organized. Get the audience seated and let the show begin.

Variation: Rehearse a fashion show in which everything goes wrong on purpose—it's fun but not easy to do. The emcee might trip over the microphone cord, or a model might come out wearing something that doesn't fit.

66

The Ladle in the Suitcase

Props: small objects (such as a suitcase, ladle, lampshade, or shoe box)

In this game, players use everyday objects to help them create silly situations. Hold up two props and ask the players to call out some situations in which they could both appear. A huge wooden ladle and an old suitcase can easily get the game going. For example, tell the players to imagine the cook of a sinking ocean liner using the suitcase as a raft and the ladle as an oar.

Divide the players into small groups and give each group two objects. Ask each to come up with their own combination plays to act out for the group. Combining a number of objects that have no obvious connection will be a fun challenge for any group.

The Treasure Map

Props: paper and pen; pirate props—such as eye patches, rub-on tattoos, wooden legs, or hook hands—are not essential but certainly add to the fun

Children enjoy drawing treasure maps showing the path to a hiding place. Ask players to draw a treasure map and bring it to the next class. Encourage them to include secret codes, symbols, hazards, and routes that are impassable. To provide some inspiration, have on hand children's books that include treasure maps or stories about pirates.

In the next class, spread out the maps for everyone to see. Divide the players into small groups and have a member of each group choose a map (not necessarily the one that she made). Ask the group to create a play in which the characters use the map. Are there pirates offshore who came to steal the map? Does the play show the search for the treasure?

68

Night Game

Props: flashlights

A darkened room is a perfect place to play the Night Game—as long as you keep in mind that some players may be afraid of the dark. A familiar story takes on a different aspect when performed in near darkness.

As a group, choose a familiar story or situation, perhaps one the group used in another game. Divide the group into pairs and give each player a flashlight. Have members turn on their flashlights as you turn off the lights. Then ask each pair to perform the story or situation while the other players shine their flashlights on them.

Variation: As long as everyone has flashlights, show the players how to spotlight a person: from the side, from behind, from above, from below, under the chin, and so forth. Have the players form small groups and make up plays using the various ways of spotlighting people and objects.

Writing in the Air

Props: cardboard or construction paper, markers or paint

Sometimes during a play or movie, a sign appears describing the location, year, or time of day of the action. The audience then knows what is going on. If the sign says "A few days later," the audience is brought up-to-date with the action. Sometimes these signs are even more effective than having a narrator, particularly when something funny is written on them, such as the POW! ZAP! CRASH! you see in comic strips.

Divide the players into small groups and ask each to create a play lasting a few minutes. Have each decide where the action can jump ahead with the help of a sign or where the action can be emphasized with an exclamation or other comment. (Transitions, which can be hard to act, are sometimes easier with a sign.) Provide art materials and allow the groups time to rehearse and create their signs before performing for the rest of the class.

Variations:

- A play can be made amusing with the help of a speech balloon on a sign board. A speech balloon contains words inside a balloon shape (like those in comic strips). A character does not need to carry the board. Stage hands can hold one up every now and then. It's often a good idea to make the balloon appear around the side of the curtain.

- Sign boards can also prompt reactions from and create exchanges with the audience. An actor might say "Oh yes, he is!" and the board, directed toward the audience, might say "Oh no, he's not!" Perhaps the actor says, "I don't see a bear," and the board (and the audience) says "Behind you!"

70

The Pie

Props: pies or cakes with cream (for throwing); old clothes; plastic sheets or a tarp; old movies

In a play, there must be a reason for every action. This is especially true for throwing pies. Although we rarely see it done today, pie throwing was very common in the films of Charlie Chaplin and Laurel and Hardy.

After the players watch some of these old films, ask them how each story line gets to the point where people start throwing pies. Then, divide the players into small groups and have each create a play in which rivals get on each other's nerves. Tell them to situate their play so that pies are available to throw. For example, two enemies might meet at a party just when the host is serving pie. As the groups rehearse (without real pies yet), make sure the actions are building up logically to a pie-throwing conclusion. Remind players that they will have to throw pies from only a few feet away to be accurate. Once the groups are ready to perform, let them put on old clothes, cover the area with plastic sheets or a tarp, and provide the pies.

Note: You can make pies for throwing by pouring shaving cream or whipped cream onto paper plates. Be sure the players know if the "pie filling" is edible or not!

The
Microphone

Props: microphone, amplifier, and speakers

You and your group can do some wonderful improvisations with a microphone and a sound system. If you have one microphone and a class of about twenty-five players, you can share the microphone in the following way.

Before class, write down several sounds that players can imitate (for example, whisper, shriek, moan, giggle, car horn, or squeaky wheel). Divide the players into groups of three and give them your list of sounds. Let each group practice a few of those sounds with the microphone in a separate room. When the groups have all had a turn, give them a theme (such as a haunted house, thunderstorm, eruption, or argument) and ask them to create their own sounds. They should also include suitable voices and a short dialogue. Let the groups rehearse their pieces and perform them for the whole group.

The Wax Museum

Props: costumes; accessories; water-based makeup; pictures of famous people, including TV and movie personalities and sports stars

Wax museums contain eerily lifelike statues. This game provides some dress-up fun for the players as they re-create their favorite people and set up their own wax museum.

Ask players to bring in pictures of their heroes, preferably full-length ones showing a pose, and some clothes or props that are appropriate for the heroes. Let the players practice the poses and then dress up like their heroes using the clothes, props, and makeup. Either you or a player can be a guide at the wax museum and dress up as well.

As a group, decide how the museum will be set up. Which famous people will be in each room? Then let the famous people rehearse how they will stand and what surprises they have in store. Have one group set up their room while the rest act as tourists, perhaps with a museum guide. When it's time to move to the next room, another group becomes the statues and others the tourists.

Two Telephones

Props: two telephones; a partition, if possible

In this game, players act out a telephone conversation. The acting is easier when players can use real phones and sit with a partition between them.

As an introduction, explain how today the telephone is indispensable—and with the invention of cellular and cordless phones, people can call anyone from practically any location.

Ask each player to create a character with a name, job, age, physical characteristics, and other traits. Arrange the telephones, chairs, and partition in front of the group. In turns, two players sit on the chairs and telephone each other, staying in character the entire time—no matter where the conversation

leads. The audience listens to the conversation and tries to discover the characters' traits and the reasons why they want to talk to someone.

Variations:

It is possible to pass the call on. If the two characters are not communicating well or enjoying the conversation, interrupt the call and let another, similar caller take his place.

Ask players about their characters, and choose two that are similar. Have those two characters talk on the telephone.

Games with Masks

Acting while wearing a mask is not a simple task. A mask partially or completely hides a person's face which means that the usual ways of expressing emotion are hidden—most people show almost every emotion through the muscles in their face. Most masks are static (they don't move when the face moves), which means that facial expressions cannot be conveyed while wearing a mask.

The advantage of wearing a mask in a play is that you are invisible; no one will notice if you blush or make the wrong expression. Players who are unsure of their own abilities often seem to act better when wearing a mask. But you can't simply don a mask and start acting. While wearing a mask, you need to exaggerate your gestures to make them clear. You also need to face the audience to convey what you want to say. Moving slowly can help you express yourself. It is also safer to move slowly, particularly if you are wearing a full-face mask.

You can buy masks at party shops, but it is much more fun to make your own. To create masks, gather art materials including the following: newspaper, construction paper, paper bags, felt, markers, paints, glitter, yarn or colored string, glue, a stapler, string, and scissors.

Meetings

Props: a basket full of masks, one for each player

Ask the players to sit in a circle and explain that they will meet each other while wearing masks. Take a few minutes and have the players develop their characters. Each player should think of three attributes for their character (for example, old, female, and happy). Have each player choose a mask and a partner. Encourage players to choose masks that represent their characters' emotions and personalities. When the partners meet, they begin a conversation about who they are, what they are doing, and where they are going.

Variation: The players should remain in character with the mask when they move to meet another player. The other player should be able to recognize who is coming by the way they move. Players can also alter their voices to suit the masks.

Feelings

Props: drawing paper and markers; camera (preferably one that provides instant photos); art materials to create masks

This drama game divides perfectly into two sessions. In the first, players practice facial expressions and create masks based on those expressions. In the second, they use the masks to create a dialogue.

Divide the players into pairs. Ask them to practice expressing various emotions with their faces. After about ten minutes, ask each player to choose an expression and draw it or photograph it with the instant camera. Have the players use the images and art materials to create masks.

In the second session, explain how players can emphasize the expression on their masks through body movements. Divide the players into pairs again and have them make up a dialogue in which both masks (and the accompanying feelings) play a major part. If, for example, the masks express anxiety and cheerfulness, the play could be about the fact that the happy character cannot understand or accept the other's anxiety.

76

More and More Exaggeration

Props: art materials to create masks

Divide the players into groups of five players each. Have each group think of a series of emotions that become increasingly exaggerated; for example, sad, amused, cheerful, and exuberant. Have each group create five masks: one for a narrator and one for each emotion.

When the masks are made, the groups decide which player will be the narrator and which will be each emotion (if possible, the players wearing the emotion masks should dress alike). Ask the groups to create a situation in which the emotions build up in a sequence of quick changes. One at a time, the players come onto the stage and have a dialogue with the narrator. The play itself should last just a few minutes. The player's movements stay the same but they become increasingly more intense. The audience watches the players, observing not only their masks but also their movements and voices.

Masks
Without
Faces

Props: masks with neutral expressions

In this game, players use expressionless masks to become as anonymous as possible. They make repetitious movements and speak in a monotone.

Choose a story for the players to enact while they are wearing these expressionless masks. How much tension can the players bring into the story? Suggest that an actor without a mask (who can exhibit emotions with extra clarity) act with a masked player to enhance the harsh contrast.

The Masked Ball

Props: costumes and different kinds of masks

Organizing a masked ball where the players may dance is great fun but requires input and help from every group member. Over several weeks, decide with the players who will decorate the room, organize the costumes, and make the masks. Encourage players to create a character, with mask and costume to match.

At the ball, each player places her character in a particular era and situation and demonstrates this either as a monologue (words and actions by a single player) or with a chosen partner. Ultimately, ask the players to remove their masks and act out the situation openly.

Games with Puppets

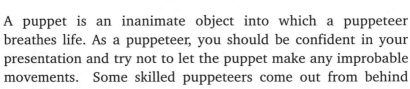

A puppet is an inanimate object into which a puppeteer breathes life. As a puppeteer, you should be confident in your presentation and try not to let the puppet make any improbable movements. Some skilled puppeteers come out from behind the scenes with their puppets and play directly to the audience. These five games, which provide an introduction to puppetry, are practice well worth the effort.

Store-bought puppets usually have a mechanical operation that is not very flexible. Encourage your players to create their own puppets, giving them characteristic postures and facial expressions.

Glove puppets need three fingers: your index finger goes inside the puppet's neck; the thumb and middle fingers work its hands. When you select or construct your puppet theater, keep in mind that it's easier to stand up when working puppets.

Remember that puppeteers don't just use puppets; they can bring all kinds of objects to life in their hands.

Simple Actions

Props: glove puppets, one for each player

This game is ideal for players who are not used to sticking their hands inside an object made of wood or soft material.

Divide the players into pairs and ask them to stand holding their puppets face to face. Have them practice basic actions: nodding yes, shaking no, looking at the other puppet, and saying hello. Ask each pair to choose five movements associated with meeting (for example, recognizing each other, saying hello, greeting with a handshake or hug, acting excited to see the other person, and bidding a fond farewell). Once the pairs have finished practicing, let them perform for the group.

A Glass of Water

Props: plastic cups and pitchers filled with water; a glove puppet for each player

In this game, players continue to practice handling puppets.

Divide the group into pairs and have each practice pouring water using the puppets. Picking up a pitcher and pouring the water can be monstrous tasks for a small puppet. Once all the players have practiced pouring water, ask them to look around the room and choose other objects (books, dress-up clothes, or building blocks) to use in a play that they will create.

Once players can handle an object well together, have them play out a probable scenario with the object that would influence the puppet's mood. For example, a drink gets spilled over a puppet's pretty dress or two puppets read a scary story.

81

Voices

Props: many different kinds of puppets

Have each player choose a puppet and then sit in a circle. Ask the players to give their puppets characteristic ways of moving, acting, and speaking. Introduce your puppet to several other puppets in the circle. The other puppets answer in character. Next, each puppet introduces himself to his neighbor on the left. Players may then ask questions of the puppets, who should answer in turn.

Ask the players to switch puppets and begin the game again. Do the players try to make each puppet move in the same way? Do the puppets get new voices each time?

Living Objects

Props: a collection of everyday objects; black gloves; black clothing, if available

Display the collection of objects and ask each player to choose one to use as though it were a puppet. Encourage players to give their puppets human names, characteristics, and emotions. Have players think about what kind of voice would suit their puppet. Is their object-puppet young or old? Rich or poor? Good or bad? Mean or nice?

Divide the players into groups of three or four and have each group make up a puppet show with their objects. Give each player black gloves, which draws less attention away from the object-puppets. Black clothing also puts more emphasis on the objects and wearing a black cap or mask over the head can make a player completely anonymous.

Human Puppets

Props: dress-up clothes and accessories

Once players have some practice manipulating puppets, let them try this game, which allows them to be the puppets.

Tell players to think about puppets they've used and how those puppets have moved. For inspiration, read books about puppets or toys coming to life. Demonstrate different ways of walking for everyone to practice together. Practice walking like a jointed doll, a very floppy clown, or a stiff wooden solider.

Have players create and become a puppet or a doll, using any props or costumes available.

Games with Costumes

Many children enjoy a game of dressing up. They try on Dad's huge coat or Mom's high-heeled shoes. With a child's imagination, a brown paper bag can become a cowboy's vest and an old dress can become a beautiful ball gown. Putting on Grandma's hat and pretending to be her or wearing pearls or a firefighter's hat—all help us pretend to be someone else for just a moment. And that's what these costume games are all about.

Garment Tales

Props: a chest full of old clothes and accessories

Ask each player to bring in a piece of clothing or an accessory that has a story behind it or on which a story could be based. Bring in your own example and tell a (true or made-up) story about it. Ask players about their stories.

Divide the players into small groups and have each group decide whether to make a game using one piece of clothing and its story or using a combination of several items. If a group can't create a play from the stories, the group members can ask the person to whom a piece of clothing belongs to act its story.

A Suitcase Full of Clothes

Props: 5 suitcases, each containing clothes, accessories, and other objects

Place the five suitcases full of clothing and accessories in the center of the room. Explain that the suitcases were delivered and no one knows who they belong to. Suggest that the players put themselves in the owner's shoes to try find out what kind of person owned the suitcase.

Divide the players into five groups and give a suitcase to each group. Ask them to create a play in which they use both the articles in the suitcase and the case itself. Provide ideas and encouragement where necessary and make sure each group discusses what will happen to the person who owns the clothes. After ten minutes of discussion and rehearsal, let each group perform for the others.

86

A Working World

Props: articles of clothing typical of a particular occupation

For this game, you and the players collect articles of clothing and accessories that convey an occupation. The group will use these objects to create a serial story.

With the group, talk about different kinds of occupations—such as computer programmer, veterinarian, baker, farmer, and others. As a group, decide on one occupation to use as a basis for a play. Talk about the various people involved in that business. For example, a veterinarian needs assistants, a receptionist, animal patients, and animal owners. Make a list of resources the group can use to find the necessary clothing and

accessories to portray the occupation (include parents, relatives, and community groups). If possible, visit the site of one such occupation for some firsthand experience.

Make up a story that includes the occupation and create a serial play (see game 53, The Serial Story, for more information). Help players choose roles and suitable clothing. Perform the play for people who work in that profession and ask if the story comes close to reality.

Long Ago and Far Away

Props: various articles of clothing depicting a specific historical period

A fun part of dressing up is pretending to be characters from a different time in history.

Divide the players into small groups and have each group choose a historical period to re-create. For inspiration, provide books that depict different historical eras; make sure they have plenty of illustrations. Have the groups research their chosen time periods, including what people ate, their jobs, the homes they lived in, and how the children were educated.

Now ask the groups to create characters based on people from their chosen historical period. Have each group compose a play about a day in the life of their characters.

88

Character Choices

Props: a wide variety of dress-up clothes and accessories

As a group, discuss different types of people and the different clothes and accessories they wear. Include discussions of different occupations, lifestyles, climates, ages—anything that influences the way people dress.

Divide the players into small groups and have group members talk about what type of person they want to play. Provide the dress-up clothing and encourage players to enhance their roles with the items.

Text Games

Our lives are swamped by words in many different ways; yet sometimes we aren't even aware of it. Everywhere we look we see billboards, advertising posters, TV programs. Books give us the strangest stories; in films, images and text transport us temporarily to other worlds; letters from all parts of the world can come through our mailboxes; a telephone call is like several lines of text through which you relate to the other person. Life without words is unfathomable.

Acting is playing with lines of text, with the ways lines can be interpreted, spoken, and people's reaction to them.

This section explains, sometimes in the form of a game, how you can interpret a fairy tale or a fable in different ways, how you can create and act out an advertising spot, how a game can be translated by an interpreter, how to hold a telephone conversation inside or outside a phone booth, and how it feels to have to write and act lines within a limited time.

Translating Words

Many compound words are fascinating if you look at them closely. Think, for example, of crossword, bookcase, or sleeping pill—all can be enacted in parts. Crossword doesn't mean a word spoken in anger; it means a word puzzle. This kind of expression can be depicted in two ways: using the real meaning or a totally different meaning.

Divide the players into groups of three or four and have each group practice acting out a few compounds. After they have had time to rehearse, let them show their actions to the rest of the group. None of the players should speak before or during the performance; the audience must try to guess the word being acted.

Variations:

- While group members are acting a compound word, they freeze on the spot and speak a sentence in which the word occurs.

- The word can also be depicted in a play (including spoken text) in which the two parts of the word are acted separately and then the entire word is used at the end. For sleeping pill, players could first use a few lines of text and action containing the word sleeping; the next part would have a few lines and actions denoting pill; and in the last sentence the whole compound would be used. The audience sees the compound word being constructed.

Act Every Letter

Divide the players into small groups and ask each one to pick a word. Tell them they will act out the word letter by letter—with each letter of their word standing for a different verb. For example, the word desk could be acted out one letter at a time with the motions for dance, eat, sing, and kick. All the members of the group act out the verbs at the same time. If the players act out the letters in the correct order, observant audience members will understand the word.

Variation: It is not essential for the audience to guess the word, so groups can act out each letter at some length. Have each letter stand for a verb that relates back to the original word. (It will not always be possible to find verbs associated with the original word. In that case, one of the players can form the shape of the letter being enacted with her body, so that the word comes across clearly. This will solve the problem and is also interesting to watch.)

Writing Together

Props: pens and several sheets of paper

Have players sit in a circle and give each one a pen. Give a sheet of paper to five or six players and ask them to write a sentence of dialogue that begins a story. When they're done, tell them to hand the paper to the person on their left. That person writes a line of dialogue continuing the story and passes the paper to the next person. Continue until each paper has about 10 to 15 lines of text on it; then suggest that the next player(s) bring the story to a close.

Divide the players into small groups and give each group a script at random. Groups read their scripts, rehearse their lines, and perform their plays for the whole group. Group members can memorize the lines, improvise them using the created story line, or use just some of the lines.

The Fable

Props: a book of fables

A fable is a story with a didactic purpose, often written in verse. Jean de la Fontaine wrote some wonderful fables about animals, such as The Raven and the Fox. In this story, a fox urges a raven sitting on the branch of a tree to sing. When the raven is flattered into singing, he drops the piece of cheese he had in his beak. The fox gulps down the cheese and runs off.

Read this or another fable to the players. Divide them into small groups and ask them to create a variation of the story. For example, instead of a piece of cheese, the raven could have a stone in his mouth that falls on the fox's head, or the branch could snap, the raven fly off, and the branch fall on the fox. Then the moral would be: If you lay it on too thick, on your own head be it.

The
New
Fairy Tale

With the players, choose a well-known fairy tale, fable, or other story. Divide the players into small groups and have each group change the form and content of the tale. For example, the story of Little Red Riding Hood could take place in the year 3000 or in prehistoric times; group members could use someone or something else instead of the wolf; Grandma's cottage could sit in the middle of a jungle or it could be a sailing ship.

Have all the groups perform their versions and talk about which ones were the most original.

94

Advertising Spot

Props: (optional) examples of TV commercials

Show a video with some TV commercials and point out the rapid sequence of images and words that advertisers use to convince a viewer to buy the products. Many players will know one or more commercials by heart and will be able to act them spontaneously—the other players will notice the fast-moving nature of the advertising spot. Divide the players into small groups and have them act out the ads in 30-second spots.

Next, have players alter existing ads and act them. Remind players that each commercial still needs to provide information, perhaps make comparisons with other products, and provide proof that this product is really better. All this has to be mixed with humor, catchy slogans, and a strong conclusion.

Variations:

- Invent a new product and ask each group to create and act out a commercial selling it.

- Once the group is used to acting commercials, ask them to perform a parody of an ad: act out a commercial but add something to make it ridiculous. There are many ways of doing this through small changes to the original. Producing proof that a product is better when it's actually worse can be even more fun.

A Different Language

Divide the players into pairs and ask each pair to create its own language—a nonsense language that they make up as they go along. This language can sound like a real one or be an adaptation. For example, instead of using all the vowels in English, players might use only A's or O's. The important thing is that the audience and the two partners can figure out what is being said.

After a few minutes, ask each pair to agree on a subject to discuss. Each pair rehearses a scene and then performs it for the group.

Variations:

- Situate the players as tourists who have to save themselves in an emergency situation in a foreign country.

- The language used can also be completely invented; it doesn't need to sound like any known language—for example, suggest that players talk using only numbers.

The Phone Booth

Props: two telephones

This game takes place in two places at once: to the left of the stage is one person using a phone; to the right of the stage is a second person standing in an imaginary phone booth. The telephone booth has a glass door which is opened and closed several times during the scene so that the audience hears only snippets of conversation from time to time.

Divide the players into groups of four and ask them to create a play in which a telephone conversation is constantly interrupted. The callers have to try to carry on despite all of the communication problems that arise.

The Restaurant

Props: tables and chairs; cutlery and plates; maybe other items of restaurant décor and costumes for waiters (optional)

Set up a "restaurant" with various tables and an imaginary swinging door leading to the kitchen. Although restaurant props are not essential, they help to create the atmosphere.

Divide the players into groups and have each group choose two or three members to be waiters; the rest will be diners. The diners should create simple conversations to use or build on when they "visit" the restaurant. When the conversations are decided, have each group in turn play the restaurant game while the others are the audience.

The fun of this game is that the conversation is made louder wherever the waiters are; if they walk away from a table, the diners' conversation becomes almost inaudible. And

if all the waiters go into the kitchen, then the audience can hear only hear their conversation in the kitchen—though the guests continue to make conversation.

In the beginning of the play, the waiters should keep their actions simple. After a while, if it is going well, they can make the action more complex. This is a game of opportunity in which rapid bits of conversation alternate with each other. Can the audience guess by listening to small parts of the conversation what the diners are talking about?

The Interpreter

This game can be played in combination with game 95 (A Different Language).

Divide the players into pairs. The first player speaks in a nonsense language and the other acts as an interpreter—he translates the first player's words as he understands them. The translations need not be the same lines that were spoken. The interpreter can also purposely mistranslate words, making the other player come across completely differently from what she intended. Encourage the interpreter to give opposite reactions to or translations of words. The interpreter can interrupt, mislead, translate incorrectly, and give answers before the questions have been asked.

Time's Up

Props: egg timer or stopwatch

Divide the players into small groups and ask each group to create a short play, which will be timed for three minutes with the egg timer or stopwatch—the play becomes a race against time. Group members discuss how they can develop the play in a couple of minutes and swiftly give it closure. If necessary, players can write down their dialogue on sheets of paper.

When the groups are ready, have each one perform while you watch the time. When three minutes are up, each play should be concluded immediately. Keep track of the timer and encourage players to quickly bring the play to an end.

Freeze-Frame Poses

Props: photographs or illustrations from newspapers, comic strips, and magazines

Divide the players into small groups and have each group choose a photograph or illustration from which they will create a play. The group must use the moment shown in the photo or illustration somewhere in their play; members decide where in the play the photo or illustration should appear. Have them practice the pose to get it precisely right. Is the pose the beginning or the end of a situation, or does it come somewhere in the middle?

Give the groups ten minutes to create and rehearse a play and then have each perform for the whole group.

Remote Control

Props: a homemade remote control

Two or three members stand frozen, as still as statues, in front of the rest of the group. They are the actors; the others are the audience. Someone in the audience says "click" or "zap" and names a television program, and the actors start playing roles from the program. After ten or twenty seconds, another person in the audience who has taken the remote says "zap" and calls out the name of another program, and the actors switch into new roles and a new story.

The actors need to know a few programs well, and tell the audience which ones they know. Whenever audience members don't like the play they can "zap" over to another program.

After a while, a different set of players takes over as the actors. Each group needs to rehearse to see if they can switch easily from one program to another. How many programs do they know and can they improvise a scene as soon as they are "zapped"?

Variations:

- The players do the same with well-known or imaginary advertisements, rather than television programs.

- The group does the same with musical programs, videos, or their favorite songs.

For More Information

Hackbarth, Judith A. *Plays, Players, and Playing: How to Start Your Own Children's Theater Company*. London: Piccadilly Books, 1994.

Schafer, Liza and Mary Beth Spann (eds.). *Plays Around the Year: More Than 20 Thematic Plays for the Classroom*. New York: Scholastic, 1995.

Spolin, Viola, Arthur Morey, and Mary Anne Brandt. *Theater Games for the Classroom: A Teacher's Handbook*. Evanston, IL: Northwestern University Press, 1986.

Warren, Bernie. *Drama Games: Drama and Group Activities for Leaders Working with People of All Ages and Abilities*. Studio City, CA: Players Press, Inc., 1996.

Index

Hunter House
DANCE AND MUSIC GAMES

....

101 DANCE GAMES FOR CHILDREN *by* Paul Rooyackers

For playing with children ages 4 and up

Part of the **SmartFun Books** series that brought you 101 DRAMA GAMES FOR CHILDREN, the games in 101 DANCE GAMES FOR CHILDREN help to develop:

- Self-esteem

- Physical coordination

- Sociability and relaxation

Guided by the understanding that the body has a special language of its own, this book encourages children to interact and express how they feel in creative fantasies and without words.

Charmingly illustrated, the dance games in this book combine movement and play in ways that release children's spontaneity and promote confident self-expression. They are organized into meeting and greeting games, cooperation games, story dances, party dances, "muscle puzzles," dances with props, and more. No dance training or athletic skills are required.

160 pages ... 30 illus. ... Paperback $11.95 ... Spiral bound $14.95

101 MUSIC GAMES FOR CHILDREN *by* Jerry Storms

For playing with children ages 4 and up

Also part of the **SmartFun Books** series, the games in 101 MUSIC GAMES FOR CHILDREN help to develop:

- Listening and trust

- Concentration and improvisation

- Group interaction and expression

All you need to play the 101 music games are music tapes or CDs and simple instruments, many of which kids can have fun making from common household items. Age levels are suggested for each game ranging from four years old to teens and up. Many games are especially good for large group settings such as birthday parties and day care. Others are easily adapted to meet classroom needs. No musical knowledge is required.

More than 160,000 copies sold in 11 languages worldwide

160 pages ... 30 illus. ... Paperback $11.95 ... Spiral bound $14.95

....

Special: *All 3 SmartFun spiral books only $39.95*

Hunter House
WORKBOOKS FOR TROUBLED CHILDREN

GROWTH AND RECOVERY WORKBOOKS FOR CHILDREN
by Wendy Deaton, MFCC, and Ken Johnson, Ph.D.

A creative, child-friendly program **for children ages 6–12,** these popular workbooks are filled with original exercises to foster healing, self-understanding, and optimal growth. They are written by a winning author team for professionals to use with children.

The Workbook is designed for one-on-one use between child and professional. Tasks are balanced between writing and drawing, thinking and feeling, and are keyed to the phases and goals of therapy: creating a therapeutic alliance—exploring delayed reactions—integrating and strength-building.

Each Workbook is formatted to become the child's very own, with plenty of space to write and draw, friendly line drawings, and a place for the child's name right on the colorful cover. Each also comes with a "Therapist's Guide" which includes helpful references to Dr. Johnson's book *Trauma in the Lives of Children* (see previous page).

Each Workbook is available as a **Practitioner Pack** for easy reproduction and a site license (call for more details).

Titles in the series include:

NO MORE HURT provides children who have been physically or sexually abused a "safe place" to explore their feelings.

LIVING WITH MY FAMILY helps children traumatized by domestic violence and family quarrels identify and express their fears.

SOMEONE I LOVE DIED is for children who have lost a loved one and are dealing with grieving and loss.

A SEPARATION IN MY FAMILY is for children whose parents are separating or have already separated or divorced.

DRINKING AND DRUGS IN MY FAMILY is for children with family members who engage in regular alcohol and substance abuse.

MY OWN THOUGHTS AND FEELINGS SERIES: Three exploratory workbooks for use with younger children (ages 6–10): FOR YOUNG GIRLS and FOR YOUNG BOYS are for problems of depression, low self-esteem, and maladjustment; ON STOPPING THE HURT is for young children who may have suffered physical or emotional abuse.

A selection of Behavioral Science Book Service

Workbooks $8.95 each ... Practitioner Packs $17.95 each

*For special discounts and additional information
please call Hunter House at (800) 266-5592*

ORDER FORM

NAME

ADDRESS

CITY/STATE   ZIP/POSTCODE

PHONE   COUNTRY

TITLE	QTY	PRICE	TOTAL
101 Drama Games for Children (spiral bound)		@ $14.95	
101 Drama Games for Children (paperback)		@ $11.95	
101 Dance Games for Children (spiral bound)		@ $14.95	
101 Music Games for Children (spiral bound)		@ $14.95	
Special: All 3 for $39.95 (spiral bound)		@ $39.95	
Please list other titles below:			
		@ $	
		@ $	
		@ $	
		@ $	
		@ $	

Shipping costs

First book: $3.00 by book post; $4.50 by UPS or to ship outside the U.S.

Each additional book: $1.00

For rush orders and bulk shipments call us at (800) 266-5592

SUBTOTAL

Less discount @ _____ %   ( )

TOTAL COST OF BOOKS

Calif. residents add sales tax

Shipping & handling

TOTAL ENCLOSED

Please pay in U.S. funds only

❑ Check ❑ Money Order ❑ Visa ❑ M/C ❑ Discover

Card # _____ Exp date _____

Signature _____

Complete and mail to:
Hunter House Inc., Publishers
PO Box 2914, Alameda CA 94501-0914
Orders: 1-800-266-5592 . . . ordering@hunterhouse.com
Phone (510) 865-5282 Fax (510) 865-4295
❑ Check here to receive our FREE book catalog

HRG 12/97